9/16/99

To Sir Daniel,

With many thanks for
your constant and enduring
friendship and support.
It means much to me.

As ever,
Your friend

Harvey

OTHER BOOKS OF POETRY
BY HARRY NEWMAN JR.

Behind Pinstripes (1984)

*Poems On Male Menopause
and Other Cheerful Topics* (1979)

Poems for Executives and Other Addicts (1974)

TURNING 21

A Businessman's Poetic Odyssey
to the New Century

HARRY NEWMAN JR.

PUBLISHED BY

NINE MUSES PRESS

TURNING 21

A Businessman's Poetic Odyssey
to the New Century

ISBN: 0-9672058-0-8

Manufactured in the United States of America on acid-free paper.

First Printing

NINE MUSES PRESS
P.O. BOX 40
LONG BEACH, CA 90801-0040

THIS BOOK IS DEDICATED TO

My dear wife Anne . . . and to
Mary, Felicity, Cathy, Alan, Ellie, and Sara.

Acknowledgments

I would like to acknowledge the following individuals for their invaluable assistance in making this anthology of my poetry possible:

Georgette "Gigi" Bradley, my assistant, for her indefatigable efforts in the prepublication arrangements and proofreading . . .

Judith Reeder of King Printing, for her inspired book design and personal interest in producing TURNING 21 . . .

Janet Wiscombe, writer, for her editorial guidance in grouping the poems and preparing my biography.

TABLE OF CONTENTS

III. NOT ALL BUSINESS

IV. ...AND THEN THERE IS LIFE

1

New Year's Poems

"I felt that holiday cards were too impersonal; so I began writing poems to mark the new year and to reflect, poetically, my hopes for the future."

R⁄

℞ for '89

May the New Year
Bring us perspective and the courage
To resist work's ceaseless demands
To break its chokehold on our lives

Let us devote ourselves selfishly
To expanding our personal time
At home, with loved ones
Or in quiet meditation

Then we can cultivate
The warmth of friendship
The capacity to love and
The willingness to be loved

Then we can laugh, have fun
Enrich the lives around us and
Accomplish the most daring feat of all

A perfect balancing act in 1989

1989

1990

NEWMAN
PROPERTIES

1990 AND OUR NEW IDENTITY

Let us make 1990
The year

> We solve our identity crisis
> Shed our pinstripe skin, snake-like
> Discard our shopworn disguise
> Discover our too-long-hidden self

> Those dearest to us are not impressed
> By Chairman, CEO, or aspiring executive
> They love us for our vulnerability
> Compassion and responsiveness
> Not for our power, money, or business friends

> We need fresh priorities and a value system
> Based on those essential human qualities
> We chose to ignore or abandon so long ago
> So let us greet the century's last decade
> Proud of our real identity—
> > Our new commitment to love and life

1990

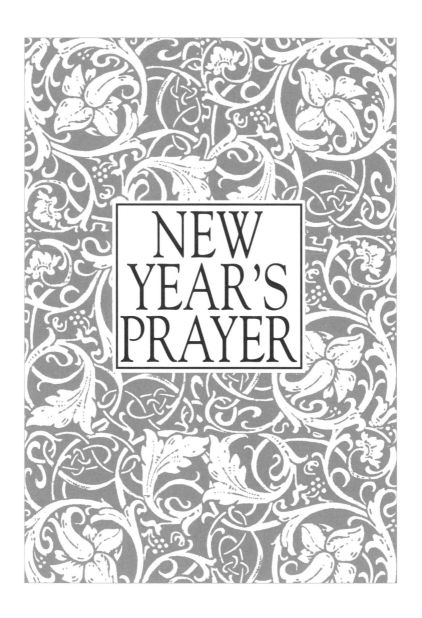

NEW
YEAR'S
PRAYER

New Year's Prayer

rant us this year
    Patience to endure hard times
    Strength to accept uncertainty
    Warmth in all our relationships
    Intimacy with loved ones
    Compassion for the unloved, the unwanted
    Tolerance for others' imperfections
    Return to handshake values
    Preference for ethics over profits
    Comfort and support of friends
    Laughter and light hearts

ay 1991 bring us closer together
    In every way

1991

1992

From My Crystal Ball

The depression has us in its coils
Wrapping itself around us boa-like
Constricting our hearts and feelings
Stifling hope and choking thought
Until the horizon turns dark, then black

We concentrate only on negatives
Crime, drugs, pollution, poverty
Political unrest, the jobless, the homeless
Desperately searching for possible solutions
But frustrated by our own pessimism

By reawakening our deadened senses
We can defeat these unnerving perils
That immobilize our will, defy analysis
We can control again our destiny
We can perceive a brighter reality

By seeing the riches we possess
The comforts of home, of loved ones
Of friendships undisturbed by externals
Of tasks, simple or complex, that absorb us
Of pleasure in touching others with our hearts

So now let us face the New Year
With courage reborn and hope rekindled
Giving full expression to our humanness
Finding in others' response to this affection
Love's ultimate reward–happiness

1992

The Gift

1993

10

The Gift

We may wring our hands - or hearts
Cry silent or unseen tears
About the starvation in Somalia
Or the senseless brutality in Bosnia
And other parts of the globe
Where ethnic cleansing stains blood-red

But we are no longer blind
To these same problems at home
In our backyards, in the next block
Gangs, drive-by murder, racial hatred
Alienated and brutalized latch-key kids
Seeking their way in a fractured world

Each of us can be part of their lifeline
In our elementary schools or elsewhere
While there is still time to instill
In youngsters from all races and cultures
Self-esteem, a sense of identity and joy
Useful skills, the ability to communicate

Only personal involvement can pierce
Our insulated lives, our gated communities
So let us volunteer our time and knowledge
To give those in need the most meaningful gift -
    Ourselves
Let that be our singular mission in 1993

1993

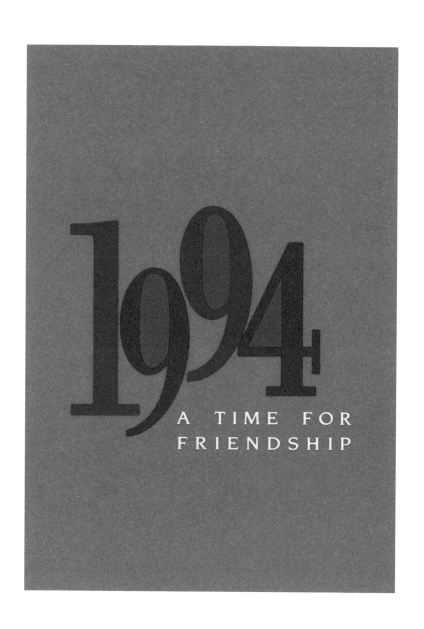

A TIME FOR FRIENDSHIP

This is not the time
To shut out a world
Fractured by racial hatreds
Bruised by economic blows
Nor is it time to withdraw within ourselves
To seek solace in depressed solitude

This is the time
To revive past pleasures
With nearly-forgotten friends
To rekindle neglected relationships
And to seek new friends
To share the warmth of kinship
Of common interests, of new pursuits
Or just the simple joy of camaraderie

This is the time
To shed our protective armor
And to open ourselves to others
Who are also searching for a seemingly
Vanished happiness and contentment

1994

COINS IN THE FOUNTAIN

1 9 9 5

COINS IN THE FOUNTAIN

We need to toss new coins in life's fountain
To replace those defaced and devalued
By our cynicism, skepticism, and suspicion that
So many politicians, businessmen, and others
Are motivated solely by self-interest

We should not be defeated
By their unconscionable acts
But more resolute in our determination
To accept what is, not condone it

It is time to tune out the negative news
To reach out and embrace those who share
Our unshakable belief in life-enhancing values
And perhaps by our example, help some
To discover the enduring rewards
Of integrity and concern for others

1995

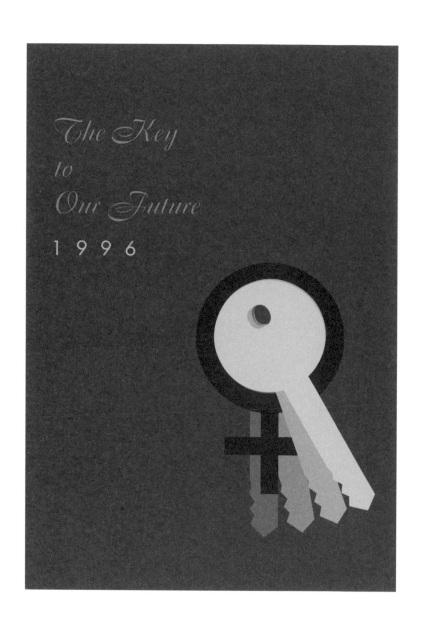

The Key
to
Our Future
1996

The Key to Our Future

Hear the voices calling
For the shattering of the glass ceiling
For the addition of their innate talents
To business and to community efforts
To salvage our foundering society
To create history's most productive merger

This synergistic melding of male and female
Will more than double our resources
Enabling us to enhance our sensitivity
To depend more on the brain's creative side
To communicate with others without words
To exercise subtle leadership through compassion

Let us embrace our newfound partners
With unabashed enthusiasm and appreciation
For what we can accomplish together
By helping society to rediscover basic values
By leading the retreat from the edge of darkness
By using the leverage of love instead of suppression

1996

NEW FACE

1997

New Face

Skeptics may scoff at Asians' apparent
    preoccupation with "face"
But let us "face" the unpleasant facts
    about our own measures of worth
We count money, power, possessions, social
    and business status as our "face"
If we unlock the vault of our own
    insecurities, face and accept them
We will have taken a major step
    toward inner peace and happiness
Then we will know that everyone on
    our Earth suffers from this same affliction
It is known as the human condition

Instead of approaching others with a critical eye
    seeking the weak points in their armor
We must risk having nothing to prove
    and accept others as they are
In this empathetic atmosphere
    without fear of duplicity or mistrust
We can escape the snares of insecurity and
    establish a new "face" for the human condition

1997

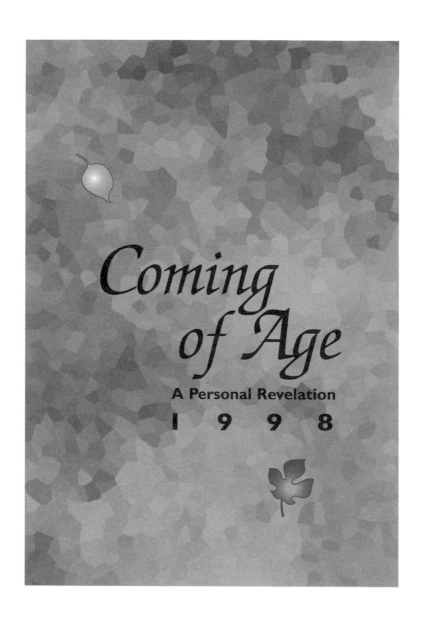

Coming of Age

A Personal Revelation

1 9 9 8

Coming of Age

Coming of Age
Is one of life's rare gifts
To those fortunate few
Who can recognize and embrace it

It is a moment in time
When past and present merge
And future becomes possible
If wisdom is unlocked

It happens most often during
Protracted illness or other rupture
Of your life's established pattern—
Then there is time to contemplate

To evaluate what has gone before—
Mindless pursuit of money and power
While neglecting loved ones
And your own inherent interests

Let the Coming of Age
Be a major turning point
In your deciding what to do
With the rest of your life

1998

1999

A New Leaf

A New Leaf

Children killing children from North Carolina to Oregon
Racial atrocities by the Texas Ku Klux Klan and others
Drive-by shootings and more gang-related violence
Genocide of the Muslims by the Serbs in Kosovo
Repeated in Turkey, Cambodia, Uganda, and Iraq
Saddam survives another U.S. missile attack
Thousands of children starve in Nigeria and North Korea
Deadly floods, earthquakes, tidal waves, and tornadoes
Presidential profligacy and impeachment
Headlines to induce nightmares, not sweet dreams

But all is not hopeless at our century's end
Warring factions in Ireland reach accord at last
Charities flourish and volunteers multiply
From the privacy of the confessional
To the supermarkets of evangelism
Worthwhile values are fervently espoused
For all of us to adopt
Whether atheist, agnostic, or true believer

Let the new century develop its own addictions
Not to drugs and another Roaring Twenties
But to increased sensitivity to personal feelings
To greater recognition of our social obligations
To increased expression of warmth and compassion
Heartfelt touchstones for all of our relationships

1999

23

2

JOINING "THE CLUB"

Testimonial

You are cordially invited
To attend, at $100 a plate
A testimonial to those
Who have devoted their lives
Unstintingly
Unselfishly
To the humanitarian purpose
Of making money

No sacrifice too great
No relationship too dear
To accumulate enough
To afford the luxury
Of giving it away
In some worthy cause
Or other

Just listen to that applause
From the thousand or more
Gathered here in tribute
Black-tied, bejeweled
Pledging their allegiance
To the honorees and
To the secret hope
That one such memorable night
They, too, might step
Into the blue-white shaft
And receive their plaque

1973

VIP, A Conversation

'I have to be there at four-thirty
For a business appointment
Before a dinner meeting
So please step on it'

'What do you do, if I may ask?'
He asked

'I develop shopping centers
Small ones, big ones with malls'

'Oh, you must really be important'

'Well, I don't know about that
How long is your shift?'

*'You're my last fare
I started just before noon'*

'What do you do the rest of the time?'

*'Oh, I go home
Only a small place
Overlooking the river
Work my vegetable garden
Go fishing or sailing
Sometimes I sit and read
Or look at the mountains*

*'I just make enough to get along
That's why it's so nice
To meet a successful person
Like you'*

1974

28

Sunday Business Trip

As the sun arcs
Bathing the senses
In its balm
A shadow spreads
Its fingers
Choking warmth and joy
From life's centrality
Of beloved faces
And familiar sounds

Another
Sunday business trip
Is there no escape from this
Compulsive mammon cult?
Will airborne sirens bring surcease
From this pain of violated sanctuary?

Through the catacombs again
To the desolate cathedral
To the crusades once more

Is my flight on time?

1974

Fear of Flying

The dull, dead litany
Of superficial contact
Between strangers on a plane
Groping for the small comfort
Of small talk
Blunts the face
Of the unfamiliar
Of the unknown
Of the loneliness
Of the unspoken
Fear of flying

1976

The Flying Shrink

At 30,000 feet or more
Two scotches and a little wine
Can make my hidden talent soar
And quicker than a wink
Transform a dull developer
Into a brilliant Flying Shrink

Though I may seem to concentrate
On analyzing 'stews'
I'll lend a sympathetic ear
To any neighbor with the blues

I'll help him see his problems
In a clear and novel light
And work out sound solutions
Before we end the flight

The only thing I hope for
Back at 30,000 feet
Is another willing victim
For the Flying Shrink to treat

1974

Out of Synch

I mark the passing of time
Not by night and day
The pulsing of the tides
The masking of the moon
The rusting of the maple leaf
The rebirth of the rose

But by appointments
Plane schedules
And deadlines
Superimposing their own
Artificial chronology
On time
And my ever-changing moods

1978

Motels

From Kansas City to Keokuk
From Tacoma to Tucson
Encased in Formica
Insulated in Naugahyde
Cheered by dime-store art
The loneliness persists

I lie in my motel bed
Listening to the sounds
From nameless neighbors
Through onion-skin walls
I think I hear
A woman's voice

My imagination flies
On erotic wings
Into warm, engulfing flesh
Before my sleeping pill
Converts the glittering stucco sky
To contrails
To numbing sleep

1974

Awake

Damn!
It's four-thirty
And I'm awake
The internal clockwork
Has sounded its false alarm

It's always the same
In Seattle, Chicago
Or New York

Like an accusing finger
The endless list unfolds
Of too much to do
And too much undone

The adrenaline of
Recrimination
Speeds the brain
The acid taste of
Anxiety
Knots my gut

The Kafka trial begins
My only plea is guilt
My defense self-doubt
My best hope, acquittal
By the hung jury of sleep

But if the past is any guide
The sentence will be suspended
Until the next indictment is returned
Tomorrow night

1973

Relapse

Waiting for another late airplane
In a faraway airport, exhausted
Unready, unwilling to face
The late dinner appointment
Expecting me to arrive

I have been here before
Far too many times
Am I here again to make one more
Deal, to earn still more money
When I already have too much?

Is it a relapse of
That old addiction—
Spinning on a wheel
In a fragmented world
In search of what?

Excitement, suspense
The illusion of motion
Or progress toward
A pointless
Predestined end?

1974

Peter, Rara Avis

A breath of fresh air
From the Midwest
Whole, wholesome, real
Warm, sociable, humorous
A sparkle in his discerning eye

How did we know
We could trust each other
With complete confidence
That we spoke with the same
Straight tongue-in-cheek

That business and friendship
Would no longer be separated
By divergent, selfish goals
That the keen sense of kinship
Would be the real treasure exchanged

1995

36

Hurry

Hurry, eat!
Down the drink
Quick, ejaculate!
Rush your work
Sleep, be brief!

Gulp each pleasure
Suck each sensation
Dry, but fast
Before such undeserved joy
Is snatched away forever

Race through life
Hurry, die!
Only by dying
Will you ever know
You were alive

It must be true
Because my mother
Told me so
And she learned it
From The Good Book
How to Regulate
The Feeding of Infants
Way back in 1921

1972

Ego Thief

He made them millionaires
But made paupers of their egos

He coveted credit for their work
Achievements and recognition

He gave them twenty-nine silver pieces
To betray their identity
Dignity and self-esteem

A modest price to pay
To perpetrate, conscience-free
The most self-destructive crime of all

1978

Button-Down Lament

What he has lost
Is buried deep within
Like Schliemann's Troy
A heritage, a culture

Tradition and the wisdom
Of Torah and Talmud
Purim and Passover
Submission and atonement

He has traded in
His yarmulke and tallith
For a Brooks Bros.
Button-down shirt

1977

The Daring Middle-Aged Man
On the Flying Trapeze

Over the awestruck crowd you fly
Floating without effort
Lazily
In circles, twists, and somersaults
Until, at last, four staunch arms
Entwine and another trick is done

The applause rises through blue-gauze air
Fills your ever-eager ears
With sounds whose inner edges
Define your shape, your being
And, fantasy-filtered, as they fade away
Whisper lullingly, 'You are a man'

The body knows in beading sweat
Underneath—oblivion
But the emptiness inside, the thickening cataract
Blinds the eye and urges you once again
To identify yourself, to confirm that you exist
Through faceless cheers at futile risks

For the enraptured masks that watch
The robot hands that clap
You live
But only as a symbol of escape
From the encrusted boredom of their cares
Their vicarious desire for *life*

1972

Success I

The illusion of success
Is a mirrored trick
Of empty adulation
Shadows of dependence
The glitter of envy
Ill-concealed

Life has no crueler joke
For all competitors are victims

The contest is how much
A goal, once attained, recedes
And the cycle begins again
And again
And again
And again

1971

Success II

I know a 75-year-old millionaire
Who has a different woman every night
And, as he waves his wallet
Says, *'They love me!'*

He owns 20,000 hotel rooms
And, they say, is worth $50 million
He pins a trick ladybug on his lapel
To attract accommodating sycophants

He adorns his walls
With portraits of clowns
Because he knows
That the contest is just a joke

1974

42

Priorities

What are my priorities—
Being nice to business 'friends'
Who might do me some good
But not to those I love
Because they understand

That all my energies
Must be devoted
Undiverted
To the world of Barron's
Where my future lies
And, of course, theirs, too?

We all must sacrifice, dear friends
I, the present to the future
They, me, to my suspicion
Of what the eternal verities
Must surely be

1974

Billion-Dollar Egos

There they sit
Enthroned on the dais
Both billion-dollar egos
Household words in their field
Dispensing their worldly wisdom
To the captivated conferees
Whose sole goal is emulation
Based on their blind adulation
Of prominence bred by success

When will they understand
What immeasurable emotional cost
What sacrifices
In close relationships
What a ruinous personal price
They have paid
For this beguiling illusion
This blindfolding chimera
The mythic city of Mammon?

1994

Business Friends

Cultivating a friend in business
Is tightrope-walking in a gale

If you have something to gain
And use your friendship
As a moral lever
For achieving it
You have placed a price tag
Of no value
On your relationship
And in the process
Made you and it, not him
A whore

If you have the strength
To elevate your friendship
Above the marketplace
And invest it with yourself
No matter what the outcome
At the bargaining table
Then you have created
Something lasting, life-enhancing
And rare

1974

Houdini of the Mind

Fantasy is the 'Houdini' of the mind
It can transform
Reality into unreality
Illusion into disillusion

Fantasy is no friend of mine
It telescopes time, distorts distances
Foreshortens life-consuming tasks
And makes distant goals seem near

Tricked by fantasy
Into overburdened reality
I strive
For that greatest of
Prestidigitating feats–
Success

1974

Marathon

My life is
A marathon dance
A crazy fad that began
When I was very young
And has been going on ever since
With its whistles, sprints, and rests

Hanging on by sheer nerve
With a body deadened by fatigue
Emotions withered by exhaustion
Clinging only to the obscure hope
That I might last long enough
To win the prize

But I am too tired
To remember what
That prize might be

1974

Hypochondria

My lower back throbs
My sinuses are clogged
And I feel dizzy sometimes
My calf muscles are stiff
My finger joints are sore
Is it arthritis?

My skin is dry and rough
From too much sun
I need a dermatologist

My vision blurs
(Particularly after wine and scotch)
My heart is beating fast

Have I slipped a disc?
Did I fly when I had a cold?
Is my jogging too infrequent?
My stomach hurts!
Could it be cancer?
My aunts had cancer
Is my heartbeat fast?
Is it arrhythmia or am I Type A
A natural for a heart attack?

It is all this pressure
In business
Deadlines, risk, anxiety
Not to mention responsibility

Hypochondria is the body's answer
To the treadmill, business way of life

1977

Wealth

Wealth is a golden albatross
Enshrined in a cage
Bedecked with precious gems
Electrified, of course
To discourage prying hands
Attached to greedy natures

It can be worn
Around the neck
On special occasions
Inspired by the need
To measure one's success
By the envy mirrored
In others' eyes

This birdlike treasure trove
Older than time
Lifeless within time
Can be acquired
By anyone skilled enough
To emulate its living counterpart
The vulture

1978

Things

The malignant appetite
Cannot be appeased
It grows
Like a consuming cancer
To fill every cube of space
With things
More things
Things upon things

New and discarded dolls
In a jumbled heap
Like babies playing Buchenwald

Television sets proliferating
Until there are enough
In every room
To watch all channels
At one time in black-and-white
And glorious Technicolor

Record players–monophonic
Stereophonic, quadraphonic
Sounds flaying sounds
Leaving no silence
Even in the inmost recesses
Of the inner ear

A yacht, a second home
Another car, paintings
Sculpture, coins, or butterflies
Each collection
Inexhaustible
Incapable
Of filling the unfillable

But the futile hope persists
That the never-ending quest
By some strange miracle
Will somehow also
Fill the emptiness inside
Or at least anesthetize
Its gnawing, corrosive hunger

No wonder holy men
Discard all their
Things
Before they can feel
Whole
Or holy

1973

Hippies

I hate those hippies
Those weirdo, freaky creeps
Doing nothing
Wandering aimlessly
Through life
Unshaven
Unburdened
Just plucking
From life's slow current
Whatever satisfies their mood
Or need that moment
And the next

You might think
Life was pointless
And all my work
Without purpose
That accomplishment
Achievement
Were not enduring
Monuments to virtue
That self-denial
Self-sacrifice, cleanliness
Were not ways to godliness!

Oh, I hate those hippies
Those weirdo, creepy freaks

1972

52

What Do You Want to Hear?
or, *The Ideal Salesman*

If I can banish my identity
And substitute his for mine
If I can play Boswell to his Johnson
And have him take my ingenuity as his

If I can be a gilt-tongued chameleon
Attuned, litmus-like, to his every mood
If I can manipulate him, unaware
To my predetermined ends
Steely-eyed above a smiling mouth
Uttering hypnotic, well-modulated sounds
Simulating warmth and understanding

Then I will achieve
The ultimate perfection
Control

And all I sacrifice
In the process
Is myself

1971

3

Not All Business

.

Felicity's Gone to College

The pugnacious headless man
The Navajo squaw doll
Hunched in concentrated silence
At her loom
Cannot see

The bushy-browed conductor
Baton poised
The ancient monk perched
Precariously on his beast
The llama and the cats
Cannot see

The fading image
Of a daughter
Dissolving in time
Through space
Absent

Feeling
For what was left behind
Only a flicker of recall
A nostalgic touch
A quick tear
A strange and distant
Familiarity

1974

Perfect Parent

Tonight I'm going to be the perfect dad
Instead of arriving home at eight
Depleted by a day of *Sturm und Drang*
I'll leave at five
As normal working people do
And much to their delight
Embrace my children
Share their joys and woes
Make myself available to join the fun

I walk in unannounced
Waiting for the shock to take effect
I recall the rush of little feet
Kisses and warm, enfolding arms
When the five of them were small

But silence greets me
I stroll into the den
Two are attached to the mesmerizing screen
'*Ssh,*' one says, holding her finger to her lips
The other waves an impatient, dismissive hand

Perhaps my son would like to play
His drums for me
But, no, his friends are coming over soon
To take him to the donut shop
Where the junior high kids hangs out

My second-oldest daughter is home
I'll listen to her practice her guitar
She has an amazing talent
May even be a genius
But, alas, she's going to a concert
Of Elton John and the Grateful Dead

'*Dearest,*' I say to their weary
Wilting, day-by-day companion
'*How about a drink?*
I think I need a double

'*Have you heard from Felicity?*
Does she like college as much this year?
No, nothing's wrong at the office
I just thought I'd come home early
For a change'

1974

Nothing to Do

'Daddy,' they say
'There's nothing to do'
Shocked, impatient angry
I suggest a multitude
Of games, activities, and sports
Undaunted, they reply
'That's no fun, Daddy'

'Then, why not be like me?' I ask
'I never have nothing to do
I always have too much to do
If I have a minute to spare
I feel uneasy, lazy, disorganized'

In short, dear children, I don't have time
To play bezique with you
(Much less to learn it)
To sit quietly and chitchat pointlessly
Or just to listen and to hear

I am so busy
I have so many important things to do
That you will grow up
And move away
Before I come to know
That *'nothing to do'*
Was a despairing plea for me

1974

Goodnight Kiss

Sara is ten

When I went in
To kiss her goodnight
I saw a dear face
So open, trusting, vulnerable
Innocent
That when I kissed
Those sweetly pulsed lips
A sense of pure joy
Welled up in me

A moment of rarest beauty
Hung quivering in the night air
Turned, and flew away

1975

Dinner with Cathy

Over a restaurant dining table
I saw her as a separate
Mature human being
Strong, forceful, beautiful
Eyes flashing
Unwilling to submit
To politesse
Or cliché

I felt uneasy
Tentative in speech
Seeking not to destroy
The fragile mood
Nor fall into a trap
Which would spring
The old response
Of no response

Cathy was always noncomformist
Upon graduation from the New-Age School
She walked down the flower-strewn steps
In cap and gown and Groucho Marx mask
To the accompaniment of her own rock band
Playing Elgar's 'Pomp and Circumstance'
She gave her parody of a commencement speech
Then parents, teachers, and students danced together

She is still the same
But different
We talked to each other
Truly interested in
What was being said
It was the first time
We had ever related to
One another that way

1976

RSVP

Squabbling is a perverted
Form of play for children
Borne of boredom
'Let me put the candles on his cake'
'Oh, no, let me!'
'Let me sit in front'
'Oh, no, let me!'

The inescapable sequence
Of maneuvering
To be number one in
The primate pack

But for me
Fatigued
Drained
By seething emotions
Imprisoned by
The straitjacket of business
It is abrasive
Rising like a siren's shriek
Piercing the ear
Searing the brain

Unleashing the flood
Of pent-up anger
Upon the hapless
Heads of those who
Unknowingly and innocently
Invite my unreasoning anger
And rejection
Of their invitation
To games
Attention
And love

1978

Dialogue with Alan, My Son

'School is just too easy for you
It's not a real challenge
Wait until you hit the big leagues'

'I suppose you want me to go
To Harvard or Stanford'

'I don't care
If you decide
Not to go to college at all
I want you to use your brains
To get a real education
Instead of just drifting through life'

'What's wrong with drifting?
You want me to be like you
Rushing through life
To see how fast
You can get to the end

'Drifting isn't so bad
It's kinda fun'

1978

Through Alan's Eyes

You think he is
Indifferent
Indecisive
Irresponsible
Irresolute

What you see as indifference
Is too much caring
What you consider indecision
Is too much analysis
His seeming irresponsibility
Is response to your judgment
He is only irresolute
Because he is seeking the truth

He is a gentle soul
But too sensitive
Constantly analyzing
Wondering if he were right
To do what he did
Agonizing over consequences

In fact, dear father
He has the soul
Of the poet
You aspire to be

1998

Three Long Years Ago

If I could stop
The ever-moving film of life
And focus on a single frame
Of Sara, sweet and ten
What would I choose?

'Doing' her ears with peroxide
The day they were pierced
The primitive ritual
Of precocious puberty?

Putting on and taking off
Her new rabbit-fur coat
A third and fourth time
Standing transfixed, hypnotized
By the mirror's admiring gaze?

Or just seeing her girlish face
Half child, half woman
Upturned
Beautiful
Innocent
Vulnerable
Unquestioning?

1978

Ellie

Antennae attuned
To every nuance
Of action or reaction
Vibrating in empathy
Or outraged by injustice
Defending the innocent
The exploited, the losers
Anyone in pain

Who has this unique mixture
Of protective impulses
And unprotected innocence?

It is my beloved daughter

1998

Perfect

I only want to be perfect
That's not too much to ask
Is it?

I don't expect everyone else
To be perfect
Only those who work with me
And my family, of course
That's not unreasonable
Is it?

When I am less than perfect
I am harder on myself
Than I am on them
When they don't live up to my expectations
Nothing could be fairer than that
Could it?

If my criticism is barbed
My sarcasm caustic
And my comments often snide
That's better than a beating
Isn't it?

The important thing is
That they should know I'm doing it
Only for their own good
And mine, too, naturally
If they know that, they should love me
Shouldn't they?

1972

What Might Have Been

Eyes
Deep-socketed in black
Insulated by sorrow
Unfocused on life
Looking inward
On bleak emptiness

Face
Furrowed by pain
Blunted by fatigue
The flash of a familiar smile
Igniting an ember of energy
For an instant
And then disappearing
Into the darkness
Of perpetual mourning
For what might have been

1972

Tears

Mined from feelings' depths
Only the double-edge of pain and joy
Can carve out these precious stones
And make them fall, tear-shaped
Down the cheek's riven path

1974

Immortality

The spurt of semen
Is a symbol
Of eternal youth
A reassurance
That the withering touch
Of age
Has passed us by
And preserved
For another fleeting moment
The illusion of immortality

1974

Stranger

I hate those cities
Because they deface me
Deprive me of my identity
Surround me with strange sights
Suffocate me in unfamiliarity

I yearn for you
Your gentle touch
Endearing words
Your comforting embrace

Isn't it strange
That these soft feelings
Well up in me
When I am threatened
With obliteration
And yet so rarely
When I am with you
Taking you for granted?

1974

Anniversary

Our love is 21
The age of maturity
Some might say
Or luck in triplicate
For the superstitious

Another anniversary
To be celebrated
With champagne
And dead emotions
By other couples

But for me
It is unique
An unfolding bud
Revealing its fiery petals
Its passionate inner beauty
Only to the sensitized eye
Of my love

For me
The bloom will never die
Nor lose its beauty
For a vital force sustains it
Against the wrinkled, spotted hand
Of withering age

It is my love for you
Deep-rooted in its own
Life-giving force
Till time becomes eternity

1975

Taking Love for Granted

Taking love for granted
Is benign neglect
It saps the energy
Leaves passions bloodless
Suffocates all feeling
Makes love an opaque memory

How can it be born again?
What spark can bring back the fire?
What chord can start the music?
What infusion can give it life?
Only your warm mouth can make it breathe
Only you can revive the heart

You never took love for granted
Only lamented its loss
In sad and quiet ways
When you felt the warmth go
You lowered the blinds around you
To dim the pain, not shut out hope

1976

Taking Love for Granted, An Antidote

Is this what they mean by
'The honeymoon is over'?

What happened to the excitement
Those vibrant feelings
Of warmth and tenderness
My perpetual desire for you?

After so few years
Is our love reduced to
Mindless habit and
Mechanical couplings?

When you asked me just to
Hold you as we lay in bed
With the waves and our breath
The only sounds

I felt a sudden surge of feeling
The welcome return of warmth
Of caring, of tenderness
Of love

Now I am alive again
I have rediscovered love
Because you always cared
And I will never let it go again

1976

Compromise

The deadly conspiracy
Of tacit compromise
Erodes marriages
Like a dry, hot wind
Sweeping away topsoil
Until the earth is sterile
And only arid dust remains

Each party to such compromise
Gives up part of himself
A piece at a time
Until there is nothing left
But desolate wasteland
Fertile ground only
For disillusion and hatred

1977

Love's Sunset

Is this the sunset of our love
A fiery circle of passion
Slipping, oh-so-quickly
Into the quenching ocean
Beyond the eye's horizon
Leaving first an afterglow
Of regret for what was lost
Then the muted grays
Of drained emotions
Until the final curtain
Of darkness and despair
Descends?

1977

Remains

'I am leaving
But you were gone
Before I left'

Whatever there was between us
In our hearts
In our minds
From our loins
Those many years
Remains
Intact
Inviolate
A part of us
Together or apart
Forever

1978

Withdrawal (*His and Hers*)

His . . .

You inflame every fiber of my being
You possess almost all the qualities I seek

And yet
I know I will find out there, somewhere
First prize for a middle-aged adolescent
In a chance encounter ordained by fate
The perfect embodiment of my ideal mate

Until then
I don't have to make a firm commitment
Or give up my self-indulgent ways
Just hear the siren call of rustling silk
Enjoy the excitement of the erotic chase
Savor the piquancy of each new face

That way
I can divest myself, banish all serious thought
Manipulate, maneuver, dissemble, conquer
Encounter them only at their seductive best
Pursue them, bed them, love them with robotic zest

And end up
Lonely, dissatisfied, an empty life
With only arid, loveless, orgasmic memories as wife

and Hers . . .

It was all you ever dreamt of
The warmth, the closeness
The intensity, the perpetual flame

But you know you don't deserve it
So turn your back on living love
Submit your resignation and retreat
Love deadness, shun pain, embrace defeat

1978

Farewell, My Love

Tonight
I said goodbye
To the passion
Of my life
With tears of love
And anguish

Tears of regret
Tears of remorse
Sentimental tears
Sorrowing tears
Tears of nostalgia
For lustful, loving hours

For peacock sunsets
In the desert mountains
In the villages of Bali
On Hawaiian beaches
At the Jeu de Pomme
On Dubrovnik's medieval walls

Farewell, my love
Let the memories
Preserve the pleasure
The reassuring embrace
Let the embers of our passion
Warm our waning years

1978

Lament for Lost Flowers

As the years float past
The roots burrow deep
Into the dark soil, spreading
Intertwining like lovers' limbs
Growing stronger, closer
Seemingly inseparable

While the once-vivid flowers
On the vines above
Wither and die
As if from some preordained
Disease imbedded
In the germinating seed

Why can't I pull out
The stubborn clinging roots
And erase forever
That hateful reminder
Of passion's spring
And love's last summer?

1978

Intimacy

Take a stand
For freedom
And you can
Know intimacy

Without freedom
Intimacy is bondage
Or its seductive twin
Love's illusion

With its timer
Set to self-destruct
When the volcanic fire
Is spent and only ash remains

1978

Love's Fantasy

Do you want me to say
I want you more than anything
That you will learn more of life
From our one night
Than from all the English classes
On romantic novels–
Even if it is a lie?

Or should I tell you
Of my need
And yours
Which are the same
Mindless flesh cry
For contact
For loving exploration
For satisfying the child
Adolescent, starved adult
In each of us–
Even if it is the truth?

I know you will
Take the lie
And reject the truth
If only to preserve
The fairy-tale fantasy of love
You vainly seek–
And never will attain

1978

Hunger

There is a hunger
Deeper than the stomach's pit
Permeating every cell
Of our being
Which cries out for
Touch
Affection
Love–
Rarely heard
And too-seldom fed

1978

Forlorn

There is a leaden quality
To the sadness
That invades my every pore
And makes me as forlorn
As a bleak English winter

The chasm in my heart
Is like a fierce wind blowing
On the Oregon coast
Haunted by its skeletons
Of gray, disfigured driftwood

Where is the sweet
Warming breath of love
To revive a freezing soul
Encrusted in the rime
Of neglect and ennui?

1977

Sexual Fantasy

We must feed
The tapeworm
Of our sexual fantasy
Endless words
Images
Sounds
But never real flesh
Or it will die

1974

Friendly Fate

Does fate bend
The ego to its will
And make of man
A fatalist?

Or does the ego
Head held high
Battered endlessly
By fear, boredom
Anxiety, pain, and
The certainty of death
Eventually admit defeat
Acknowledging thereby
Its helplessness
Its vulnerability?

By such surrender
Man can find new strength
To seek the love, the warmth
The understanding
And fulfillment
The desperate need for which
He has so long and hopelessly
Denied

1977

Deep Massage

Her psychic hands explore me
And stop without apparent cause
Like a scientific ship
On its maiden voyage of discovery

Every eddy, whirlpool, unexpected spume
Crosscurrent, outcropping of rocks
Which breaks the rhythm of the waves
Is a signal for her to stop and probe

She finds debris at every level
Bits and pieces, discarded, destroyed
Last week, last year, decades ago
And brings them to the surface

Her subconscious sonar sounds the depths
And defines a giant and hoary mollusk
Whose muscle opens and as suddenly
Closes to guard its hidden secret

Then the wrecks; small boats
Derelicts, hulls, a veritable fleet
Of sunken destroyers and men-of-war
From many battles lost in earlier days

Next the razor-sharp underwater reefs, unseen
Capable of inflicting terrible pain
Nurtured by their own self-generating poison
Spreading, growing
Providing homes for brilliant flashing fish
But impeding the tides, the currents' flow
A gross, beautiful excrescence of the deep

Finally
The treasure-trove
Frozen in the depths
Perhaps from decades past
Untouched by time
Except for the sea's tireless surge
To set it free

Heading back to port, the first trip done
But the expedition only begun
The hands aboard feel good
Rewarded by their efforts
And the sea is vibrant
Its surface shimmering
In the sky's last darkening rays

1977

Instant Intimacy

We cry only for ourselves
Our sadness, loneliness
Or relief
At making contact with another

We taste the salty wetness
Of each other's tears
To ease
Our thirst

We feed on each other's body
To still the hunger
For affection
Touch and intimacy

And thus remain
Separate
Apart
Alone

1977

Male Menopause

What strange demon
Assaults the sanctuary
Of the middle years
Convulsing that even tenor
Of single-minded tedium

With its garter-belted
Black-stockinged, slit-skirted
Braless, skin tight invitation
To the last dance
We missed so many years ago

To the meat market
Singles bars, the discos
Friends of friends, wives, widows
Divorcées, secretaries, mistresses
In a blind, mindless search

Driven by compulsion's need
To rekindle fires
Of extinct excitement
To recolor gray passions
Tumescent purple

Wife, children, business
Friends, home, old comforts
Whatever the cost
It is not too much to pay
For one last gasp of life

Or its seducing illusion

1977

Second Marriage, Anyone?

Feel the fear
The terror
Of commitment
To the unknown
To the unknowable

Tremble
At the threat
To privacy
To freedom
To identity

Panic at the prospect
Of cloying companionship
Of stifling intimacy
Of emotional demands
When you cannot respond

But do not hide them
In the dark closet
Of sleep
Or the deadening fatigue
Of work

Or you will
Never know
If you can
Face the risk
Of real relationships

1978

94

Hold Him Gently

Hold him tightly
Don't let him get away
Remind him a million times
How much you love him
Play the *'adore you'* game
In the hopes that
He will do the same

Let anxiety be your compass
Insecurity your guide
And he will soon
Be gone
Forever

Hold him gently
Let feelings be your tongue
No need for words
Your eyes convey the message
Your fingers trace the flow
Your presence brings ease and comfort
Fans affection's warmest glow

Let independence be your compass
Self-confidence your guide
And he will soon
Be always
By your side

1983

My God, I'm 60 and Time Is Running Out

My God, I'm 60
And time is running out

A frenzy seizes me
My limbs tremble with desire
My heart palpitates with hunger
For whatever love I can find
In this painted jungle
Filled with lithe young huntresses
In their skimpy loincloths
With their superficial, single-purpose minds

My God, I'm 60
And time is running out

I will throw principles and purism
To the Indian-summer winds
And clasp the unthinkable compromise
To my neglected, yearning breasts
I will settle for brutish lust
And sacrifice my intellect
To any woman who can satisfy
My baser, more basic needs

Because I'm 60
And time is running out

1983

First Impression

The death-mask of fatigue
Hides disfigured dreams
Of romantic love

The bitter burden of reality
Crushed schoolgirl expectations
Of happily-ever-after endings

Now the ceaseless stream
Of cosseted, abrasive egos
Beleaguers your identity

Only the fleeting smile
Salvaged from the guarded recesses
Of your undernourished heart
Lets me glimpse the reservoir
Of surging love, emotion, and desire
Straining to be set free
To finds its joy-fulfilling destiny

1984

Cri de Coeur

How can I deal with
This unquenchable thirst for love
This insatiable hunger for affection
Which disrupts my days
And bedevils my nights?

I stand alone
In the heat of burning deserts
In the chill of frozen arctic waste
In the dark of subterranean caverns
Drowning in the murky ocean depths

Is this just another blip
In the uneven tenor of my life
Or a potent reminder
Of unrealized goals
And the desperate need
To find meaningful ways
To be an achiever once more
And deserve to be loved again?

Clearly, I must learn to
Love myself for who I am
Not for my accomplishments

1983

Honeymoon Hymn

Honeymooning in Kauai, an oasis
Of romance and passion flowers
Where the sun envelops us
With its radiant warmth
And the romantic mist screens us
From our physical surroundings

Communicating by sound and touch
Without words, our emotional waves
So attuned that spoken words
In any language
Could not fully express
What we have to say

1984

Our Vacation Is Over

Our vacation is over
And all we leave behind
Is fourteen days' of bliss
Of exquisite intimacy
Laughter, easy conversation
Of affectionate touches, knowing glances
Games, books, and childhood memories shared
Of sunset walks along the beach
Sun-filtered searches for tropical fish
Of rapturous embraces repeating
The ocean's pulsing beat
Of love's flowering

Our vacation is over
Real life begins tomorrow

1984

Lady Luck

In the dark, steaming
Jungle of my emotions
A brilliant shaft
Cuts the darkness

The tigers' snarl and the
Monkeys' piercing shrieks
The elephants' thunder and the
Sharp-edged shrill of the birds

These sounds are
Suddenly stilled by
This strange aura
This miracle of love

The meshing of emotions
This merging of moods
The confluence of feelings
This unity of passion

All are a paradox
No more than a lucky break
Dependent upon the
Random roll of the dice

1984

Love's Alchemy

Making love to you
Is a religious experience
I feel an exaltation
A glow of transcendental faith
An overwhelming sense of union

If God is love
Invest hedonism with God
And transform it
With the alchemy of love
Into pure gold

1985

Memorial On Highway 19

'*Lianne loves David*'
'*T.R. loves Keilani*'
Heart-shapes capture
Other coupled lovers
To remind posterity
In pure white stones
That they, too, have had
Their volcanic hours
Of molten passion
Which, like the lava flows
Have cooled and congealed
Into the fissured tedium
Of real-life relationships

1986

Escape to Paradise

The heavy-lidded lethargy
The sun-drenched somnolence
The sloughed-off skin of cares
Moldering in equator's heat
Mark the midpoint of escape
From remote responsibility

Can it be that I am free
That time is now timeless
Measured only
By the tides
Revealing and concealing
Their iridescent coral?

Sunrise and sunset etch the islands
In a pink and black prelude
To Jupiter and the Milky Way
Schools of luminous fish
Dart in the cobalt blue lagoons
Re-enacting the Darwin drama

Fijian drums and serenades
Summon us to feast
And seek nepenthe
In the kava bowl
As we bask in the
Bounty of 'Paradise'

If I truly deserve
To enjoy myself
Why is it so hard
To escape
And why do I feel
This flicker of guilt?

1986

Love Cocoon

Love is like a cocoon
That wraps its silken web
Around us until we are
Shut off from the world

While we are locked
In the warm embrace
Of perpetual passion
Too absorbed to notice

1989

Blessed Balance

Prudery spawns prurience
Prurience breeds indiscriminate sex
The notorious one-night stand-offs
Where two people get together
But miraculously never connect

This is the malignant formula
Which undercuts our society
Debases the role of women
Enhances gross male chauvinism
Stimulates the wrong in the religious right

Oh, for the blessings of balance!

1995

Afterglow

Suffused by love's afterglow
I could cry out for joy!
Every fiber of my being
Vibrates with pleasure
At the memory of kisses
Embraces, loving words
Silent endearments
Repledging our troth
Replenishing ourselves
With life's most potent force

1997

Welcome Home

Love's greatest reward
Is the return of the loved one
Without you, my life was barren
Every day, every hour overcast
With gloom and isolation
Redeemed only by the prospect
Of your return and our sunlit time in Kauai

While you climbed Montana mountain peaks
Watched geysers gush their innards
Hiked to the edge of exhaustion
I knew you were shedding
The endless burden of daily chores
The constant attention to my needs

You needed the time to contemplate
To analyze your feelings in a fresh setting
To decide if your life was frozen
In a loveless, desiccated pattern
Or whether you could still recapture
A caring, fulfilling relationship

Could you renew the marriage vows
With their dual commitment to trust
Or would you have to settle
For a nagging uncertainty
Adding to your already overburdened life?
You can only wait and see

1998

Anne Is 'Poipu Perfect'

This Hawaiian sojourn reminded me that
You are unsurpassed at every level–
Intelligent, devoted, tender
Helpful, supportive, considerate
Empathetic, literate, honest
Trusting, forgiving, affectionate
Unselfish, modest, brave
Fastidious, sensitive, patient
Loyal, tolerant, dedicated
Charitable, artistic, gracious
Thoughtful, generous, compassionate
Responsive, playful, kind–
You are unique and irreplaceable
My partner, my beloved

1998

Love's Anne-versary

Sweetheart, after our honeymoon in Hawaii
I thought it would be impossible to
Recapture the intensity of that
Passionately moving experience
But, the impossible has occurred

Now, 14 years later, I find that
My love for you is deeper and
More profound than ever before
And I understand more clearly
Why and how I love you

Many of the endearing qualities
That I have learned
To recognize and respect
Are captured in the verses
Of 'Poipu Perfect'

But I have seen them even
More clearly during my illness
Your caring ways and willingness to
Sacrifice your own needs to
Comfort me are beyond measure

Your inner and outer beauty
Shines like a beacon constantly
And has helped to define
The nature of my
Overwhelming love for you

1998

4

...And Then There is Life

Alone (In Prospect)

I have never been alone before
And I am 51 years old

Monks in monastery cells
Hermits in desert caves
Recluses in brownstone mansions
Make a career of it
Yet I have never been alone

The prospect transfixes me
With fear, anxiety, apprehension
Modified by curiosity
At what answer it will give
To questions till now unasked

What if no one is there
When I arrive?
If he really does exist
Will he be as boring
As I expect?
Will he be of shapeless lead
Or of a lighter alloy?

Will I find joy and peace
And warmth with him
Or just a mutual pact
To count the hours restlessly
Until it's time to leave for home?

1972

Alone (In Retrospect)

Sixty hours alone
Are not eternity
But an opportunity
To introduce yourself
To you
Not as reflected
In other people's eyes
Nor defined by others' words
Emotions or reactions
But just as you

'Who are you?' and
'Who am I?'
Are the same, I discovered

I found peace and
Contentment with me
Anxiety and apprehension
Moods as variable
As the morning sun
Making its hesitant way
Through the bay fog
Moods as changing
As the sounds of
Children's voices and barking dogs
Motorcycles' whine and shifting gears
Throbbing engines and bird songs
Rising in waves
From the valley below
Punctuated by the shrill insistence
Of the foghorn cry
From the distant sea

Once the 'you' and 'I' had merged
In newfound friendship
Based on self-loving and respect
There was something more
To alone

A sense of unreality
A hint
Of what might have been
And still could be
A severing of human contact
With others, or oneself

And, more disturbing still
A reminder
Of what will inexorably be
The ultimate alone–
Death

Did I say
Sixty hours alone
Are not eternity?

1972

Chicken

I love to play chicken
I'll tell you how it works

You accept each dare
To perform an ever-more
Dangerous feat until
At last your courage fails
Judgment outweighs pride
Or your body quails
At the prospect of pain
Disfigurement or worse

At which point you lose
Because you are chicken

My version is a little different
I test love and life
Until I discover the borderline
Of loneliness and death

At which point I withdraw and win
Because I am chicken

1973

Just In Time

He was always pressed for time
But now he is not
Because he is
As they say
No longer among the living

Now he is free to enjoy
His family
Hobbies, TV
And all his other
Things

His heart attack was
As they say
A blessing in disguise

1973

Why Is Life So Untidy?

Life is untidy
The neat packages
Keep coming undone
And the pigeonholes
Change shape
As I try to push
The damn things in

I can't understand why

When I was eight
I could make a perfect part
Get every hair in place
And it took only 32 minutes

1973

Trying

Don't try, they say
Let the feelings flow
Naturally

Trying cuts them off
Like an aborted baby

So I try not to try
But it doesn't work
So I try *very hard* not to try

Until I realize
What I am doing

Then I try not to try to try
Not to try to try
Not to try to try

Until the feelings of futility
Flow naturally

1973

An Artist's Soul

A persuasive voice
Diguises his artist's soul
As it entreats the muses
With pensive pleas
To inspire his mind
With true enlightenment

While his conscious self
Pampers his outer being
With ambition's potent weaponry
And his ever-restless soul
Quests to feed
His spiritual needs

1974

Hang-Ups

All of us
Have hang-ups

We nurse our insecurities
With arrogance and false assurances
Envying qualities others have
While scorning or ignoring our own

Desperately seeking contact
Yet tongue-tied by clichés
Emotions paralyzed by fear
Thwarting *'to love or be loved'*

Neurotic undercurrents can carry us
Willfully resisting or passive
Into the whirlpool depths
Of unreality

I have been there
And everywhere
A fellow human being
Suffers failure, guilt, or pain

Because I share
Some part of it in me

1974

Love

Upon its entry into the world
Baptized in the holy water
Of the withdrawing womb
The baby's head is crowned
With perfection

Created in Thy image
Unformed
Innocent
Vulnerable
Feeling
Craving
Love

The cord is severed
The trip begins
An unholy consecration
From perfection
To corruption

The form distorted
Innocence debased
Vulnerability violated
Feelings denied
But still craving
Even more desperately
Love

1974

124

Love's Straightjacket

Our prudish society and conformist parents
Impose a sraightjacket on love
Restricting its expression
To the outworn Victorian dictum
That it is proper to love only one
With guilt the price of any digression

When we respond to a friendly voice
Or feel sudden rapport at first contact
Or develop a closer relationship
Based on deepening mutual respect
Or recognize a profound kinship
Which transcends sexual bounds

We should unlock our emotional chastity belts
And be free to expose our true feelings
With a loving look, an affectionate embrace
An honest statement of our attraction
Only then can we exercise our newfound sensitivity
And fully appreciate love's many subtle distinctions

1974

Before My Time

To have aged
Before I am *old*
Not like a vintage wine
With its smug bouquet
Basking amber-lit
In candle-glow

But like a pitted retread
Worn smooth
On a '53 pickup
In a Long Beach junkyard
Is just the way
It is

1974

Criticism

Criticism is a cutting tool
Razor-sharp and diabolically designed
For demolishing egos
Eviscerating gut reactions
Cutting the props of self-confidence
From others and oneself

Criticism lays down barbed wire
Around the personality's perimeter
Warning potential trespassers
'No human contact wanted here!
Keep out!'

In one stroke, it can reduce
An equal or superior
To Lilliputian size
Stifle a conversation
Strangle an inquisitive mind
Suffocate a free spirit

Force the emerging social chrysalis
Into the straitjacket of conformity
Harpoon, paralyze, demoralize
Anything original, creative
Or unacceptable

It is dangerous
In the hands
Of the immature

For the cynic
The skeptic, the ambitious
Or, worst of all
The insecure
It is a lethal weapon

1974

Am I Alive?

A glimpse of death
A breath of oblivion
Invests life with life
Cloaks being with reality

Why this endless testing
This dabbling in the art
Of self-destruction
Except to prove
That I am alive?

1974

I Cannot Hear My Heart

The doctor placed his watch
Next to my ears, in turn
'Can you hear it?'
He asked gently
'Yes,' I replied

But I cannot hear my heart

It speaks louder
Than the gentle ticking
Of a watch
It talks of feeling
It is spokesman
For my body

Yet I will not listen
And so
Must pay the price
Such fatal deafness exacts

1974

Reminiscences

Is reminiscing an admission
That the past
Shaped by memory's distortions
Is better than
Reality's pain
Here
Right now?

1974

Reunion

Time fades
A decade disappears
In the warmth
Of friendship renewed

The nostalgia of laughing times
Of easy companionship
Of shared experiences
At the struggle's start
Becomes reality again

The glasses clink their toast
Not for something that is past
But for a new surge of feeling
That is with us now
Comforting, enveloping
Whispering, *'I feel at home'*

1976

Here and Now

Today is yesterday's
Anticipation
Tomorrow is dissatisfaction
With today's
Expectation

A painful process
Repeated endlessly
Until anticipation vanishes
And each day
Has its own identity

Then and only then
Can feeling have reality
Then and only then
Will I be here
When it is now

1976

Newman's Law

Insurrection is often
Resurrection
Hegel had it figured out
Eighty years ago

All-night poker games
Three-day drunks in Boston
Moving from right to left
Or radical to reactionary

Rebelling against
Authority of schools
And parents
Or government
Or anyone, anything
Telling you what to do

Rebellion
Is a declaration
Of selfhood
But it is not freedom
It is prison
In a perverted form

1976

Lost Innocence

The skin sags and wrinkles
With age and exposure
To the elements
And the passing years

But not so quickly
As idealism and innocence
Have been eroded
By exposure to my fellow man

1976

Death of A Friend

Friends are more than people
They are reference points
For past experiences shared
They revive the feelings
Of the event even when
The memory is fading

It is so painful
When a friend dies
So much of the reality of
Your life dies with him

1976

Hang-Gliders

Like prehistoric birds
The hang-gliders
Float on aircurrents
Beyond the cliff's edge
Etched by the sun's
Bright, dappled seascape

Moving more quickly
Than the lengthening
Shadows of Torrey pines
Or solitary golfers
In their programmed pursuit

The gliders fade
Into the sun's blinding path
Neither daring nature
Nor defying death

But uniting with the elemental
Ebb and flow
In joyful, soaring surrender

1977

What Others Think

Why not let
What others think
Dictate
How you behave
And what you enjoy?

Then you are certain
To be rewarded
By avoiding their criticism
Or, better still
Their disapproval

That way, too
Life will slip by
Before you find out
Who you are
And what brings you joy

Or even who *they* are
Who manacle
Your life

1977

Self-Destruct

Every human emotion
Carries within its womb
The seed of destruction
The hunger for approval
Can force concessions
Bury anger and eventually
Deny the very feelings
Which gave it birth

The lust for power
Can inflate the ego
Till there is no room for
Empathy, for feeling
Only the ability
To see others
As impersonal instruments
To use and manipulate

1977

Hubris

Pride is a stage-set
Made of flimsy canvas
Painted in strident tones
Its only support
Spindly struts
Which tremble
When a door slams

Its windows
Looking out on
Sunlit meadows
Elegant old streets
Or the eaves of Montmartre

Whatever landscape
Fits the script
The ego creates
With infinite pains
But behind the facade
There is only
Emptiness

1977

Pre *est*

Your instant intimacy
Your crass camaraderie
Prevent the natural process
Of human contact

You may covet the world
With your impersonal embrace
Your billboard smiles
Your glib, synthetic words

But your pious-robed ambitions
Will eviscerate love
Destroy its subtle hierarchy
Debase its value
Leaving only the dross of selling
Where deep and meaningful relationships
Might have been

1978

Panaceas

Like snake-oil salesmen
Praising their patent cures
For all of human ills
Speaking in tongues
Of psychobabble
Christianity reborn
And murky mysticism

Erhard, Graham, Hubbard
Maharishi, Moon, and
Countless modern prophets
Push their panaceas
To the multitude
With hip, hypnotic hype

Attracting crusaders
To their cause
Of more crusades
Providing purpose
For rudderless lives
In a tumultuous sea
Of tidal-wave expectations
And dark-wake disillusion

1978

Expectations

I was taught in school
That life is logical

That love is
Good behavior's reward

That material success
Is hard work's end product

That honesty and/or integrity
Will be recognized and applauded

That raising a family
Is the *summum bonum*

That dedication to a goal
Will bring joy and fulfillment

That people are reasonable
And behavior rational

But I have discovered
In the ruthless rush of living
That the only rational thing
Is the ability to describe
Define and accept
The irrational
Which is life

1978

Cat Envy

Curse the cats who lie there
Curled up quietly
Soft, furry, tactile
Not wanting anything
Except a soft resting place
In the warmth of the sun
Or the fire's reflected heat

Women pet them
Stroke them gently
Cuddle them tenderly
Fondle them lovingly
Talk baby-talk
Until they purr
Their insouciant pleasure

What one consciously seeks
One never gets
That is the lesson
I will not learn
From cats
From Zen
From life

1978

Faith

If I believed in God
I would pray to Him
To preserve the last vestige
Of my innocence, my naiveté

If it should be destroyed
By the same dark forces
That have eroded it
Through fifty-six years
Of disillusioning experience
With my fellow man
That last strand of faith
In human nature
Would be destroyed
And, with it, me

I envy those who can draw
From their spiritual wellspring
Of unquenchable faith
In something other than
Fallible, finite
Man

1978

Self-Importance

There is a strange illusion
Of importance
Which attaches us
To the world
Like an uncut
Umbilical cord

We think we can
Reshape human nature
That others depend upon us
For happiness or existence
That life could not
Go on without us

Until time erodes
This insistent fantasy
And experience merges
With reality
To wither the cord
Until it falls away

1978

Traitor Eyes

Sometimes I wish I had
A two-way mirror
So that I could look
Through the face
That others think is mine
Without their knowledge

And watch their reactions
To the games I play
The strategies I use
The adroit maneuvering
The subtle manipulations
In short, the human engineering of them

I would take pleasure
From their frustrated efforts
To discern my motives
To pierce the shield
Of clothes and manners
Voice and gestures

But there are two traitors
To this fantasy of mine
Which perceptive eyes can probe
And discover all the secrets
Of my mind, my heart, my soul–
Thank God!

1978

What If?

We plan a pattern
Of events
As if we were in control
Of life

But then things happen
Or fail to happen
As if by chance
Or design

Leaving us only
To celebrate or
Bemoan our fate
And prolong the
Illusion of control
By speculating
'If only' and
'What if?'

1978

Judgment

If only I could suspend judgment
Until the Judgment Day

Or step down from the bench
Without passing sentence on mankind

If I could stop using the microscope
To seek the spirochetes of human frailty

Or pull off the long, black hood
And let them recognize the executioner

If I could blunt the razor's edge
Of my criticism's guillotine

Or enjoy the passive and performing arts
Without the need to find perfection

If I did not have to feel superior to others
As an antidote to not respecting or loving me

Then I could be happy, at peace with
Myself, and love my fellow man

1978

148

The Troubled Fifties

The fifties are a troubled time
When what has gone before
At times seems joyless and
More often, futile
An endless succession of the same
With no prospect for relief

The fifties are a troubled time
When lifelong careers are shucked
Like a snake's dead skin
And decades-long marriages
Founder on the rocks of boredom
Borne of too many compromises
Too many trade-offs
So that no feeling is left

Nothing remains
After the children have gone
To start the cycle once again
With the same high hopes
We once had
Thirty years ago

The fifties are a troubled time
When most of us are too frightened
To admit that life is finite
And the end is closer
Than it was

1978

Journey's End

My ship is in
With riches in the hold
The excitement of the voyage
Of barter and battles
In alien lands
Has faded into memory
And fatigue

Did I map its course?
Was I ever at the helm?
Or did some unseen force
Fill the sails
Control the currents
And guide my ship to port?

If all that remains
Is to find safe storage
For my treasures
And to stand guard
Then launch the ship again–
Brave new hazards
And threatening seas, I say!

Or this will be
My only journey
To journey's end

1978

Retirement

'Retire,' they say
'You can afford it'
But would I have an identity
As a nonentity
Scribbling verse
Puttering with books
Getting to know myself
And others around me?

Better to weave an
Intricate web of relationships
Full of love, warmth
And communication
Achieving fulfillment
Instead of
Fulfilling achievement
Which is ego's illusion

1978

New Horizon

The bright horizon
With its infinite promise
No longer beckons me

Now I see only the sun
And the thin line in the west
Towards which it moves, imperceptibly

I wish it could be dawn again

1978

Final Years

Close the blinds
Shut out light
Spurn the world

Live within the
Self-imposed prison
Of arthritic pain
Migraine headaches
Urine bags
And all the other
Plaques imposed by
Age on the aged

Preoccupied by pain
Relieved only by the pleasure
Of outliving peers
Of token giving to the poor
Of patronizing menials
Of sacrificing themselves
Oh-so-nobly to one another
They fretfully await the end

I hope I will find better ways
To spend my final years
Than they

1978

Lonely Old Man

I don't want to be
A lonely old man
Unwanted
Unmissed
By those supposed
To love me

Neither father
Nor husband
Only rejected
Rejecting child
Replaying the part
Long after the cast
Has disappeared
And the lines have become
Just hollow sounds
In an echo-chamber life

1978

Anger In Disguise

Sarcasm is anger in disguise
An insidious, manipulative tool
Used by unlettered louts
To express raw resentment
Or by arrogant elitists
To mask their real motive
A mocking insult disguised by guile

1984

Sternklang

Klang, klang, klang
Gong sounds
Resonating, vibrating
Voices in and out of harmony
Aware yet oblivious of one another

Flutes, conch shells
Temple gongs
Calling the faithful
From their reverie
To the startling incandescence
In the still night air

White-clothed messengers
And musicians
Etched by torch smoke
Singing their strange
Cacophonous harmonies
In the forest glade
To the screeching obligato
Of the toucan and macaw

The mad synthesizer
Answered by the tuba
And the trombone
All congealing into one
Mesmeric chorus

The roar of the beast
The assault of the dark winds
The thunderclap breaking
Its dissonant showers
On those in the thrall of
The hypnotic flame

156

The staccato sounds
The shrieks, the groans
Are all fragments
In this outer space of life

Earthly and unearthly
Worldly and unworldly
Spiritual and hedonistic
Religious and atheistic
Kaleidoscopic impressions
Fragmented thoughts
A thousand vibrations
Fleeing through the black air

And suddenly
There is no end

1984 Olympic Arts Festival

Anne's Lament for Her Cat

These damp cheeks
These red eyes
These tears
Are for you, Boo

You were always there
To bring me comfort
To snuggle on my lap
To look inside my heart

Now you are dying
And I can scarcely bear the pain

Is this my final warning
Never to need again
Never to love too much
Never to cling to another?

Or is this sorrow
A blessed revelation
Of the small price I pay
To love, to be alive?

1985

158

Smile

A smile is like the sun
After a bleak December day
Its radiance melts anger
Hostility and intolerance

It unlocks the vaults
Of vulnerability and affection
It reassures insecurity
Offers sanctuary to shyness

Bridges the awkward gap
Between fearful strangers
Extends the hand of friendship
In a frightened world

Like an electric charge
Smiles spark emulation
Ignite the encrusted heart
A smile is the face of love

1986

Life's Shadow

The creak of ancient bones
The pain of knotted muscles
The cautious, halting walk
Are all signposts of age
Which we cannot disguise

Secretly envying young bodies
But unwilling to acknowledge it
Or the ghost hovering in our brain
Reminding us of immortality
And its darkening shadow

1994

The Inner City

The home of hope and despair
Of glittering high-rise offices
Exciting theaters with art, music, and dance
Or ugly erosion of what once was new
Dirty, infested, poverty-stricken slums
Where overcrowded families eke out existence

From the energy of renewal and power
To the lethargic dance of poverty's attrition
Add the diversity of cultures and languages
And from this cacophony of sounds and meanings
A regenerated inner city will emerge
More vigorous and vital than before

1996

Russian Roulette

Is witnessing a moment in history
More exciting in retrospect
Than the experience itself–
The statues of Lenin being dismantled
Yeltsin atop a Russian tank exhorting
The crowds to back his power play?

Yet to watch the long-suffering queues
Waiting silently and shuffling patiently
To buy their modest daily needs
From dark and scantily-stocked stores
While feeling hope for the future
Was both moving and depressing

To visit Kiev's Babi Yar Valley
Where Nazis massacred thousands of Jews
To hear the frightening accounts
Of the Chernobyl nuclear disaster
To see neglect corroding Leningrad's gilt edge
Left me disenchanted and disheartened

What I experienced seven years ago
Was positive and life-enhancing
Compared to today's
Economic collapse, corruption, and
Desperate struggle of the masses to survive–
Perspective redefines reality

1998

Mirrored Man

Images are my reality
I exist only in the mirror's eye
Reflecting each persona
I choose to project on it

One is the charming
Debonair man about town
Another is the self-assertive
Successful business tycoon
Yet another is creative, literate
Perceptive and sensitive

The innovator
The generous, benevolent benefactor
The critical, pedantic perfectionist
The talented discussion-group leader
The pillar of virtue and integrity
The roué antic, passionate lover
The convivial, gregarious partygoer
The witty, irreverent raconteur
The indiscriminate flirt
The impatient, irascible boss
The articulate, introspective poet
The lady-lover, lady-killer
The insecure, unloved little boy
The incurable, everything-is-possible optimist
The person who always needs to be in control
The lonely man at the top
The Harvard-Cambridge intellectual elitist
The conservatively, meticulously dressed aristocrat
The frustrated jazz pianist and dancer
The critical, sarcastic ego eviscerator

1998

Insecurity In Control

The need to control
Is the measure of insecurity
To direct the fate of others
Is the strength-inducing drug
Creating an illusion of superiority
To the subservient sycophants
Submitting for self-serving reasons
To the domination of a mordant autocrat
Whose strength disguises weakness
And a sense of inferiority
Matched only by uncertainty
And a lack of faith in himself

1998

Warehouse of Memories

My mind is a memory bank
In which I store all experience
Impressions, pleasure, pain
Each incident in my existence
From the first gasp of air, the birth cry
To the riddle of last night's dream

But the computer is down
There is a grave short-circuit
In the aging mechanism
Constantly erasing memories
That can never be recovered

I wish I lived in a warehouse
Where I could store every scrap of
Paper, every photograph, every
Conversation, every book, newspaper
And magazine I had ever read
Exact images of all the people
I have known
Furniture, scrapbooks, pictures
Of every place I have lived
Memorabilia from every event
I have experienced

Then there would be no doubt
That I had lived

1999

Agnostic–Genius or Fool?

Is an agnostic Narcissus reborn?
One who feels no need for explanation
Of the endless miracles of creative nature
Its seasonal variation from green to white
Its surging seas with their teeming netherworld
The mysteries of snow-capped mountains
Verdant valleys and cactus-dotted deserts?

Some agnostics are not awed by trees and flowers
The jacarandas brazenly disporting their purple
While the oleander bushes beneath compete
With their red, white, and pink plumage
Even Mondrian could not duplicate
The infinitely varied patterns of leafless branches
All under the vaulting, arching firmament
A universe studded with countless star-planets

They accept it all without question
As part of their personal stage-setting
Is it arrogance, ignorance, or stupidity
That blinds them to the inevitable realities
Of birth, life, and death?
Perhaps, when the end is near
They may express surprise or disbelief
That the gyrations of their existence
Of their loving and hating relationships
Should be taken for granted

These agnostics are either unaware or too frightened
To pose the basic questions–
What is the source of life and death?
Is there a power greater than mine?
Who ordains it and guides it all?

Other agnostics may pose these same questions
Searching for answers in Darwin's theory of evolution
Or other scientific explanations of their existence
They may also conclude that there is no answer
Which they can identify and verify
That the sole course of action
Is unquestioning acceptance of reality

This approach does not discourage
Consideration of others and a virtuous
Moral and decent personal lifestyle

These lives guided by the Golden Rule may be even
More common than the crude, insensitive
Self-centered existence attributed to agnostics
Especially by their pious counterparts

How do agnostics view religion?
Are the religious simple fools
With a blind belief in some supreme power
God, if you will, or some other identity
Inspired by divine revelation to one

Then passed on from generation to generation
Leading to unswerving faith and worship
Of Jesus, Buddha, or other East or West messiah
Who guides the devout in multiple ways
To cope with, understand, and accept
An otherwise inexplicable universe?

The simple answer is
There is no answer
You must choose

1999

Reincarnation

Old souls
New souls
The fortune cookie says
We will live again–
Is life a fantasy
A delusion
A blind search
For fulfillment?

Is one life span enough
Or must we return again
To create, destroy, heal or poison
In our Da Vinci or Hitler guise?
Who are we
And what is our destiny–
How will we know it
When it arrives?

Must we search
Through space and time
Or will we find
Contentment
In a child's touch
In music or laughter
In a woman's love
Or kinship with a friend?

When we satisfy others
Do we fulfill ourselves?
When we own a surfeit of things
Why is that not adequate?
Why do we achieve a goal
And shatter it ourselves?
Why is enough or too much
Never enough?

Is reincarnation the chance to find
The magic formula to change fantasies
Into illusion or reality?
Am I here again to repeat these
Futile efforts to create for humanity
Something I cannot do for myself?

My soul is seeking what
I have not been able to find
In this or past lives–
Constant love and attention
To share, to cherish
To preserve forevermore

If I can achieve this
Let this be my last incarnation
Because then I can leave fulfilled
And my tired body
Will at last surrender
To eternal peace and joy

1995

5

P.S. AUTHOR PROFILE

HARRY NEWMAN JR.
Biography of a Shopping Center Pioneer and Poet

by Janet Wiscombe

From his perch on a chair in the dining room of his contemporary waterfront home in Southern California, Harry Newman Jr. surveys the trappings of his impressive success as shopping center pioneer, and poet. He is talking about business developments in Asia, and is struck with an idea.

"I'm going to call it 'The Great Mall of China,'" he deadpans.

A mischievous smile travels over his face. He is a humorist who loves language, an entrepreneur dedicated to education, an innovative executive more likely to quote *Winnie the Pooh* than Warren Buffet. Newman is a Harvard- and Cambridge-educated bard whose tastes currently run more to free verse than bottom lines.

Beauty and humor are necessities in the life of this passionate, complex man, but it is ideas and people which capture his heart and mind. On the one hand, he is a practical, down-to-earth businessman with handshake values. On the other, he is a poet with a creative mind, and, in earlier times, a bon vivant with a fondness for fine wine, custom-tailored suits, and, even once in London, top hat and tails.

Those who know him best describe him as a visionary who does not allow the tasks of the day to eclipse his concern with the future. He is known for anticipating trends and for contributing original research to the academic study of business. As co-author of the text "Teaching Management," and the founder of the British Case Study Writers' Circle during his eight years in England, Harry produced the country's first case studies on human relations. In the United

States, he was the first chairman of the International Council of Shopping Centers' (ICSC) Educational Foundation, and initiated the nation's first case study research on shopping centers. These studies have been used to develop graduate-level programs for colleges and universities throughout the nation. He is also well known for research in the group-discussion method, and for creating new ways of doing business that emphasize customer service

"In business, timing is critical," he says. "To be successful, you have to understand that each situation and each personality is different. You must have foresight, the ability to project what will happen, and the imagination and willingness to take a risk."

> If I can be a gilt-tongued chameleon
> Attuned, litmus-like, to his every mood
> If I can manipulate him, unaware
> To my predetermined ends
>
> Steely-eyed above a smiling mouth
> Uttering hypnotic, well-modulated sounds
> Simulating warmth and understanding
>
> Then I will achieve
> The ultimate perfection—
> Control
>
> And all I sacrifice
> In the process
> Is myself

Throughout his career, Harry has softened the edges of the more pragmatic world of business by writing and by actively participating in numerous civic and cultural activities. He has served as adjunct professor of real estate development at the University of Southern California's Lusk Center, and as president and chairman of a number of organizations, from the Long Beach Opera to Cedar House, which is a much-emulated program for abused children and their parents. As chairman of ICSC, he testified before the U.S. Senate Finance Committee on the Tax Reform Act on behalf of the organization, which now has 37,000+ members.

Most importantly, he has committed himself to education—from developing innovative business methods, to providing cultural opportunities for poor children. Following the Los Angeles riots in 1992, Harry was so deeply troubled by economic and racial chasms that he immediately plowed resources and time into after-school programs for poor inner-city children. He enlisted the help of other professionals—from businessmen to journalists—to teach classes. He taught a class in poetry. The project was an extension of the Regional Arts Foundation, an organization he had founded a decade earlier, which provided opera performances and other cultural events for low-income elementary school children.

In his own poetry, Newman writes about corporate life, the price of success, loneliness, raising kids, divorce, illness, male menopause, second marriage, love. During the years he traveled extensively, Newman often composed poems on airplanes. He is a man with a taste for plainspoken prose. "I like straightforward language that deals with emotion," he says. "I have no real academic interest in poetry. I like self-revelatory poems." He wrote about saying good-bye to his first wife. He wrote about divorce, and his second marriage to his beloved Anne. He wrote about the impact of his work on his children.

> Tonight I'm going to be the perfect dad
> Instead of arriving home at eight
> Depleted by a day of Sturm und Drang
> I'll leave at five
> As normal working people do
> And much to their delight
> Embrace my children, share their joys and woes
> Make myself available to join the fun
>
> I walk in unannounced
> Waiting for the shock to take effect
> I recall the rush of little feet
> Kisses and warm, enfolding arms
> When the five of them were small
>
> But silence greets me
> I stroll into the den—
> Two are attached to the mesmerizing screen
> 'Ssh,' one says, holding her finger to her lips
> The other waves an impatient, dismissive hand

Perhaps my son would like to play
His drums for me
But, no, his friends are coming over soon

'No, nothing's wrong at the office
I just thought I'd come home early
For a change'

Harry is a seeker, a student of the human condition and of his own frailties. "I never thought I was good enough," he says. "That self-doubting led to being a perfectionist and an overachiever."

The story of Harry Newman Jr.'s unlikely odyssey from the Midwest to Cambridge University, from sales pitches to poetry, begins in St. Louis, Missouri. He was born September 22, 1921, in the wake of the Great War and the destruction of the Old European Order of his ancestry.

Harry is a man who embraces the two distinct cultural sensibilities of his generation: an old-world respect for classicism and tradition, and a new-world appreciation for innovative ideas and for indigenous American cultural and art forms such as jazz and baseball. As a kid, he served as assistant bat-boy for the St. Louis Cardinals, the year the team won the pennant, an electrifying experience. He still remembers the lineup: "Sunny Jim Bottomley, first base. Frankie Frisch, second base. Tommy Thevenow and Rabbit Marinville, short-stop. Andy High and Sparky Adams, third base. I wore a Cardinals uniform. It was big time."

During most of his childhood, the Newman family lived in a grand brick house with a castle tower. Harry attended private schools, and was awarded a scholarship to Harvard. Even then, he had a reputation for charm and humor, and was a natural at bringing people together.

His mother had a passion for elegance, art, music, and intellectual accomplishment. His father traveled a lot, and was not as available to his

176

children as they would have liked. Harry fell into the same trap. Now he is making an effort to recapture what he missed.

> I am so busy
> I have so many important things to do
> That you will grow up
> And move away
> Before I come to know
> That 'nothing to do'
> Was a despairing plea for me

Harry's upstairs office is a sanctuary filled with a rich array of family pictures, and shelves crammed with books ranging from treatises on opera and humor to novels by Charles Dickens and Tom Wolfe. The space above his desk is reserved for his most-prized personal memorabilia: a picture of Cambridge University, where he attended graduate school at St. John's College in the late '40s, and a 50th reunion photograph of the Harvard class of 1942.

Newman's prestigious alma maters define what he most cherishes: education, tradition, sophistication, excellence. For this natural-born student, the college years were of enormous academic and social significance. During his freshman year, he quickly established himself as a thinker and creative organizer. As campaign manager with classmate John C. Lacy, he mapped out a campaign to elect Lothrop P. Withington class president. Harry invited the press to the Harvard Union dining room, where he had arranged to have Withington swallow a live goldfish. The incident touched off a national goldfish-swallowing craze.

Newman, a German literature and language major, joined the literary Signet Society. But it was the tremendous energy he put into redesigning and "revolutionizing" the Harvard Album that permanently whetted his appetite for the world of writing and publishing.

He was also deeply committed to community service. Harry not only taught a drama class at Trinity House in East Boston but, as President of Phillips Brooks House, the Harvard Center for *good works*, he recruited a record 1,000 Harvard undergraduates to teach at settlement houses and boys' clubs, and to distribute food to the hungry.

 On Sunday morning, December 7, 1941, Newman was 21 when he heard the fateful radio report in his room at Adams House: *Japanese Attack Pearl Harbor.* The world convulsed, and Newman's generation went to war. He was able to complete his studies before he was drafted into the Army and sent to Aberdeen Proving Ground in Maryland, where he spent the remaining war years, and where he wrote for *The Flaming Bomb*, a military newspaper which attracted professional journalists to its wartime staff. His passion for words continued to flourish, and he was eventually named editor of the publication.

After his discharge from the Army, he returned to Harvard to inquire about postgraduate studies abroad, and was advised to apply for Cambridge University on the G.I. Bill. In 1946, he and a crop of bright young Americans set sail aboard the Cunard Line's *S.S. Washington.*

It is his legacy as editor that keeps the name Harry Newman alive at the 600-year-old institution. In 1947, he and his friend Geoffrey Neame started a weekly college newspaper called *Varsity*. The general-interest publication was the university's first campus newspaper, and has survived and prospered for half a century.

The ink on his Master of Letters degree from Cambridge barely dry, Harry and Geoffrey Neame began publishing beautifully designed and printed books, brochures, and maps: from literature for the British Arts Council to the first Fodor travel guides in Europe.

Harry married and returned to the United States in 1955, first to New York, then to Southern California, where he began leasing retail space. He quickly anticipated a need for small combinations of stores where customers could buy donuts, get their hair cut, clothes dry-cleaned, and shoes repaired in one place. No one had thought of clustering small service-businesses together in mini-malls before, and Newman's idea gave him a distinct competitive edge.

Still, it was a tremendous adjustment for the young family to relocate from a vibrant London life to an uncertain future in California, where a big night out was grilling a couple of 39-cents-a-pound chuck steaks on a backyard barbecue. He eventually opened his own firm, Newman Properties, which specialized in commercial development, leasing, and management. His debut into ownership was a neighborhood shopping center which featured the first Sizzler Restaurant.

By the mid-seventies, Newman was the father of five, and was developing large enclosed regional malls and other centers from Orange County to Seattle-Tacoma. In all, he developed more than nine million square feet in California, Washington, Nevada, Texas, and Iowa.

"Money has never been a consuming interest," Harry says. Although he cannot deny he enjoys the trappings of a financially successful life, he says, "Most people are confused about wealth and the importance of power. What's important in life is your personal value system. What I find worthwhile is warmth, affection, friendship, kindness, generosity, influencing other people's lives, being thoughtful of other people's needs."

> *If you have the strength*
> *To elevate your friendship*
> *Above the marketplace*
> *And invest it with yourself*
> *No matter what the outcome*
> *At the bargaining table*
> *Then you have created*
> *Something lasting, life-enhancing*
> *And rare*